Penny for Your Poems

Penny for Your Poems

Claire Nicholls

Published by www.lulu.com

© Copyright Claire Nicholls 2018

PENNY FOR YOUR POEMS

All rights reserved.

The right of Claire Nicholls to be identified as the author of this work has been asserted in accordance with the Copyright, Designs and Patents Act 1988.

No part of this publication may be reproduced, stored in a retrieval system, or transmitted, in any form or by any means, electronic, mechanical, photocopying, recording or otherwise, nor translated into a machine language, without the written permission of the publisher.

This is a work of fiction. Names and characters are a product of the author's imaginations and any resemblance to actual persons, living or dead, events and organisations is purely coincidental.

Condition of sale

This book is sold subject to the condition that it shall not, by way of trade or otherwise, be lent, re-sold, hired out or otherwise circulated in any form of binding or cover other than that in which it is published and without a similar condition including this condition being imposed on the subsequent purchaser.

ISBN 978-0-244-07764-8

www.clairenicholls.co.uk

Book formatted by www.bookformatting.co.uk.

Contents

Penny for your poems..1

Feelings 2

My love 3

Jealously 4

Don't look back 5

Growing older 6

Your worth it 7

Panic 8

Stop 9

Your gone 10

I want 11

Choices 12

Believe 13

My mind 14

Love 15

Happiness 16

Dreams 17

Moving on 18

Determination 19

The survivor 20

Smile	21
Worry	22
Scared	23
Anger	24
Calm	25
Sadness	26
Loneliness	27
Sleep	28
Friends	29
Reflection	30
Thoughts	**31**
Stories	32
The palette	33
The canal	34
Sunny days	35
Secret	36
Sunrise	37
Rainbows	38
The Church	39
The Cavern	40
Space	41
Flowers	42
Music	43
The Hunter	44
Looking	45
The candle	46

Footprints	47
Fire	48
The web	49
Shadows	50
The ocean	51
Spring	52
The wonderer	53
Wind	54
Time	55
The storm	56
Memories	57
Stillness	58
Rain	59
At night	60
One day	61

Penny for your poems

Penny for your poems
I would like to share with you
Some are happy some are sad
They might relate to you

Why don't you write down how you feel
Don't be ashamed to let it out
For it's important that we do
You will feel better without a doubt

For your story might inspire someone
Maybe years from today
Help them feel like they are not alone
To guide them on the way

We are only human
We make mistakes and have wobbles too
If only we talked about mental health more
See it's not just happening to you

Feelings

Be grateful for your feelings
Happy, scared or sad
For that shows you are alive
Life can't be all that bad
Happiness comes in different forms
Just look and find it there
Dig deep, look within your soul
And find it nestled somewhere
Everyone gets sad
Some more than others
It can go deep within your bones
You may find it even smothers
Being scared means you are being brave
Through choice or maybe not
Push through it won't last forever
Let it out don't let it rot

My love

Hurry home my love
I'm calling out your name
I need to feel your warmth on me
Before I go insane
Hurry home my love
I have a restless heart
It needs to feel you next to me
I hate it when we part
Hurry home my love
My eyes are just for you
You are my one true love I say
For you I'll always be true

Jealously

Grumbling inside and my mood is feeling low
Trying to hide it but I think that it might show
I feel like I am falling while others are just fine
Wish I could switch off this jealously of mine
I want to be as good, successful and succeed
Instead of getting engrossed full of my own greed
I should be admiring with positive vibes
Just can't help thinking they have better lives
Pick myself up, and stop the self-loathing
I'll achieve nothing if I sit here and keep moaning

Don't look back

Please don't trip over your future
If your too busy looking back at your past
That's happened its gone let it go
It was never meant to last
For now, it's just for today
That you should focus on
Before you know it's gone in a heartbeat
Today will already be gone

Growing older

Sometimes I stand and look upon
The mirror on my wall
The face that stares right back at me
I don't recognise at all
My face has got that bit older
My hair is different too
My eyes I guess are still the same
Staring back at me so blue
Inside my head my mind is still
As youthful as before
It just takes me a little bit longer
To get ready and get out the door

Your worth it

Look inside your mind and be inspired
See inside your heart and feel loved
For you hold the key to your happiness
Your amazing just hold your head up
Don't worry that you are different
It's better to stand out on your own
Don't compare yourself to others
Set yourself free and just grow
You and your thoughts are important
Find what you enjoy and don't quit
For no one else can make you happy
Look inside feel value your worth it

Panic

I close my eyes to block out the light
My head is spinning, and I feel so light
Every noise I hear, starts to intensify
Creating pictures from sounds
My mind just cannot lie
Skin starts to prickle, hairs start to ripple
Breathing speeds up fast, I feel like it's my last
Then slowly there is a change. A breeze comes drifting by
Grey clouds have passed and there is blue within the sky
A coolness spreads around, the danger now is gone
Time to return to normal and then carry on.

Stop

Stop, stare
What just caught her eye
A million silent whispers just came floating by
Barely touching her skin, enough to make her shiver
Like sun sparkles gently on the ever flowing river
Hardly visible to the naked eye
The emotion made her want to cry
They held onto secrets, some untold
A few were over a hundred years old
Trying to absorb into her skin
Let them pass though on the gentle wind

Your gone

I thought about you lots today
It felt like you were near
I often think I'm doing ok
But then I shed a tear
I wonder if you're watching me
Are you still around
I wish you could just let me know
With a white feather or a sound
Sometimes when I awake
I forget that you have gone
Then I feel it deep inside
Your passing was so wrong
I will keep a safe place in my heart
Where you will always be
For now I will just have to be strong
I hope your proud of me

I want

I want to feel the rain
Falling against my skin
Soothing this feeling
From deep down within
I want to feel the sun
Beaming down on me
To warm this frozen heart of mine
And let me be happy
I want to feel the wind
Rushing through my hair
To make me feel alive again
Do things without a care
I want to feel snow
Tingling on my nose
Become a child and make snowmen
Until I can't feel my toes
I want to feel excitement
Adrenaline rushing by
Make my heart pump faster
My life rush before my eyes
I don't want my life to pass me by
Wake up and feel too old
I want to feel everything
Stand up and start being bold

Choices

It was only when she was at her lowest
She could see how far she had come
Time after time she had built herself up
Once again she was feeling numb
She yawned and stretched and pondered life
Choices what she thought were right
The need to find a place to be happy
Shut away darkness, turn to the light
For remember nothing lasts forever
Try and make peace with today
For it is the start of something new
Bring out your inner child and play

Believe

Time to put on your positive pants
Today we start the day
Chapter one of your story starts
Make those demons go away
Find one small positive thing
About the life you live
You don't even have to love it
Just appreciate your here
Get your blood pumping here we go
Feel the fresh air touch your face
Start with a walk just 10 minutes or so
Take your time it isn't a race
Make yourself a glass of water
Put it on the side
Every time you have a bad thought
Take a glug, feel the coolness inside
Make a list of things you need to do
Tackle them one by one
Even if you only do one again
Soon they will be gone

My mind

You keep me awake at night
With your tune of lonely songs
Please switch off and let me rest
Why ask me to right my wrongs
Draining me of energy
Daylight has almost arrived
Today is going to be such a long day
I'm so so sleep deprived
Some days your full of determination
Positive thoughts flow through
But others you seem to not want to function
I can't seem to get through to you
Just remember I'm your master
I take back control you see
I'll distract you and make you forget
You will never have power over me

Love

There are Butterflies inside of me
I'm grinning from ear to ear
Heart skips a beat when I hear your name
I go giddy when you are near
I'm happiest when we are together
You're the perfect company for me
I hate it when we have to part
It makes me get all teary
You share a piece of my soul
I'm feel peaceful when you hold me tight
Love that has come from a billion lifetimes
You grace your presence in my dreams at night

Happiness

Is happiness waking with a smile
Or having a good night's sleep
Perhaps it's a warm summers day
Or arranging friends to meet
Is it eating your favourite food
Washed down with a hot cup of tea
Maybe watching trashy television
With your pet snuggled up on your knee
Maybe it's having time alone
Reflect and catch up with your thoughts
I think it's a balance, a pinch of it all
It's something that can't be bought

Dreams

I'm looking forward to falling sleep
I have an appointment with my dreams
The one place I can be whoever I want
I shut my eyes and hear my heart beat
Sub conscious mind come out and play
What's in store for me tonight
Will I famous, rich and pretty
Or will I be in for a fright
Pieces of memories get all jumbled up
Playing at different time frames
Memories of past join up in the present
Play tricks on me silly mind games
Waking up I'm quick to recap
The delight of my dreams once more
Write them down quick or gone forever
Lost deep into your minds core

Moving on

She nervously kept checking the time
Knowing she had to get out of this grime
This could be the start she was looking for
All she had to do was walk through the door
Excitement made her skin prickle up
No more drinking from the remorseful cup
Glancing around the lifeless space
She really had to leave this place
Step by step towards the door
Her body said stop, her mind craved more
Daylight dripped through the tiny door crack
Slamming the door behind no looking back

Determination

Falling at the first hurdle time after time
Wanting to quit this stupid idea of mine
It won't work, I can't do it I shout out loud
Voices within say make yourself proud
Digging deep inside trying to be brave
Shutting off opinions of what others say
Time to believe in myself once more
Be bold as a lion, hear that roar
All the doubts make them vanish
Irrational thoughts time to banish
One life here so need to shine bright
Hard work determination make it right
Focus on my goals don't give up
Books don't get written with just luck
I will make this happen I will achieve
Satisfaction will be guaranteed

The survivor

Standing alone in a field
She had never felt this alive
The wind against her face
She felt that she could fly
Inhaling the air into her lungs
Her arms stretched to the side
But she couldn't leave the ground
All she could do was cry
She felt like a broken angel
Whose wings had been clipped
A piece of the puzzle was missing
Like a beautiful vase that had chipped
But she knew she was repairable
Although a scar it would leave as a gift
She was a survivor, a warrior, a woman
Her emotions now would start to shift
Sensing a change was coming in the air
She knew she could feel it in her bones
Opening her eyes, she was soaring high
She knew she was never really alone

Smile

Smiles can be contagious
Try and you will see
It can light up someone's day
It always works for me

For you never know someone's story
They might feel really sad
If their journey now takes a different path
I'm sure you would be really glad

Worry

Twisted knot inside of me
Getting tighter all the time
I look back at my reflection
Wish it wasn't mine
I'm not feeling hungry
But to the fridge I go
Not idea what I've been eating
Only empty packets will show
Endless hours spend worrying
On situations that don't really matter
Wish I could share with a friend or two
Have a coffee and really good natter
But time to change my mindset
Turn bad situations on their head
Replace a bad one with a good one
Rest easy at night in bed

Scared

Goosebumps appearing
Heart is getting quicker
Hairs on my neck are standing up
Lungs are feeling thicker
Fight or flight feeling
Adrenaline starts pumping
Don't know whether to sit or stand
My head is really thumping
Ok so I'm scared
Not afraid to say
Bravery pushes its way through
Here to save the day

Anger

It builds up inside, want to let it out
Trying to keep it in, think I'm going to shout
Like a pressure cooker, bursting at the brim
Everything annoys you, got to keep it in
Blood is like it's boiling, feel it in my veins
Got to get out of here, need to halt the reins
Please just give me a minute, just on my own
Let me chill out, go into my own zone
Put on some music, dance without the sound
Now I'm feeling ok. I'm ready to be found.

Calm

Breathing is steady
I'm not feeling edgy
Pulse isn't racing
My body isn't aching
Palms aren't sweaty
I'm not saying help me
What is this feeling
I don't know it's meaning
Is it calm I wonder
I sit down and ponder
My mind tries to ignite
As I think of what it's like
It's too relaxed to care
I'm feeling as light as the air
Don't overthink this good time
I'm going to claim it as mine

Sadness

Tears roll down my face
I have no reason why
Sometimes I shut myself away
Just sit in my room and cry
It's easier than explaining
Why I feel this way
Got to pull myself together
Have to carry on with my day
No one can see what I'm feeling deep down
Unless they look into my eyes
But I tell them I'm fine, there's nothing wrong
I cover it all with lies
Until one day I pick up a pen
The words spill out, I'm trying
When I open my eyes the paper is full
I realise I'm no longer crying

Loneliness

It stalks you in the background
Keeping out of sight
Then hits you when you least expect
Engulfs you with all it's might
You try your hardest to keep it at bay
Distraction is the key
Sometimes that just isn't enough
You sit there thinking why me
Talk with others, share your story
There is always someone who will understand
A problem shared, is a problem halved
Be your greatest fan

Sleep

My head is on the pillow and I'm twisting and I'm shifting
Trying to get to sleep tonight but I'm not even drifting
The hours go past one by one, It's not even funny
Birds are waking from their sleep, soon it will be sunny
Whoever said sleep was easy, clearly has no idea
Swap places with me for a day or two and all will become clear
My eyes are getting sore, from rubbing them with my hand
My head is going to explode like the tide crashing on the sand
Daytime has come around, far too quick again
Maybe tonight's the night that sleep will be my friend.

Friends

Friends can be like angels
Pick you up when you are down
They are a shoulder to cry on
If you ask they will come around
Sensing when your unhappy
Always there for you
They will always have your back
When your feeling blue
A note of caution though
Choose your friends well
If you pick the nasty ones
They can make your life hell
Friends are like natures medicine
Make you happy when you are sad
Take care of your friends, look after them
Be the best friend they could have

Reflection

Look deep into your soul what do you see
Gaze through your eyes relax and breathe see that person staring back at you
That reflection in the mirror
Most of us wish we were fatter or thinner
And it will come as no surprise
If you were to look through everyone's eyes
Other people's heads are full of mixed emotion
But not everyone decides to show them
We are human after all
And get back up after a fall
A good day is great
A happy day is better
Push through the pain
You have everything to gain

Thoughts

Stories

Why don't you delve into a book
When you have a spare hour or two
You won't regret it you'll be hooked
Doesn't matter if they are old or new
Be transported into a different place in time
Make the characters become your friends
Use your imagination and expand your mind
The possibilities never end
Find something that you'll enjoy
Let your brain electrodes spark
Magazines, books, it doesn't matter
Listen to an audio book in the dark

The palette

Vibrant colours, clean and solid
Awaiting the swift gentle brush
Will it be thin and delicate
Or tickle the palette quite rough
Blending and absorbing in turn
Colours collide and begin to smother
A different colour emerges
Slowly evolving from each other

The canal

Man made but with a natural beauty
Quite stunning for all to see
Carved into the land twists and turns
The only place that really calms me
Narrow boats chug along
Your never ending path
Bright colours adorn the floating homes
With names that make you laugh
Working boats are far and few
No longer needed to carry supplies
Some are beautifully preserved
A really rare treat for your eyes
The atmosphere is so peaceful
The pace has been turned down slow
If I won the lottery and had to choose
This is the place that I would go

Sunny days

Great big ball of fire in the sky
Starts waking, rising slowly way up high
Warms up the land makes everything glow
Sunny days make me smile when I'm feeling low
Your scorching beam making everywhere bright
Flowers turn their heads just to see your light
Penetrate my skin fade away my woes
Spending the days outside anything goes
Soothe my worries send them away
Shine on forever don't go please stay

Secret

Tell me your secret
Spill your guts to me
I won't tell anyone
It's between you and me
I'll keep them safe
My lips are shut tight
We can share it together
It will make you feel light
Share your words silently
Let my mind fill up some more
For I am the keeper of stories
That's what I'm craving for

Sunrise

The darkest dark of nights
Will soon start to fade away
Night creatures take their final flight
To hide from the light of the day
Look far beyond the horizon
A spec of light emerges
A huge ball of fire prepares to arise
Bringing light and warmth as it surges
Twilight fades away it's silvery glow
The atmosphere changes all around
In its path the sky turns golden
Its silent but alive with a rainbow of sound

Rainbows

Thick torrents of rain angrily fall
When will the clouds finally empty
The earth is so wet from all your tears
The trees and the flowers have had plenty
A great ball of fire comes blazing through
Roaring into the dark grey and explodes
Mother Nature collides, brings colours to my eyes
From your amazing great shield of rainbows

The Church

The silhouette of the church
Stands silently behind the trees
Guarding souls as they sleep
Upon the gentle breeze
The bells ring out from the tower
Echoing around at night
Sounds vibrating across the countryside
Giving night creatures a fright
Your windows look inviting
Your door carved with beautiful wood
The grand design is magnificent
Oh, the secrets you could tell if you could

The Cavern

Deep within the icy cavern
I bravely go and explore
What of this strange new world
That even the sun rays won't pour
Stories are hidden out of sight
Behind the velvet green moss wall
Beyond the depths of the world I know
Pillars of stalagmites stand tall
Adventures I will embrace without fear
Spine tingling at possibilities
Air feels different somewhat magical
Beneath the earths facilities
Onward I go and wow what do I see
Shading my eyes as the glare is bright
A beautiful lake spread out so far
Filled with gems in a rainbow light
As I draw close I feel their energy
Wondrous colours float above
Reaching out I fall into the air
Filling me up with light and love

Space

Never ending inky blackness
Lit by stars along the way
Past planets and craters shooting stars
This is where I want to play
Chase around moonbeams
Hide and seek in a black hole
Let's get lost amongst the planets
Up here we are in control
Exploring far off galaxies
The earth looks so far away
Let's spend forever exploring new worlds
It's so beautiful everyday

Flowers

The flowers are gone
It's all black and white
Nothing to look at
It's a terrible sight
No red and no yellows
Just gravel and dirt
Can you feel the pain
I'm feeling the hurt
For they have been stolen
Haphazardly pulled from the ground
No one saw anything
Taken without a sound
I hope it now pleases you
With the flowers in your jars
For they will now die slowly
The beauty that won't last

Music

The beats are vibrating through me
It's travelling into my soul
Through my veins into my head
For tonight I'm on a roll
I'm dancing in the dark
My eyes are shut so tight
I want to block out all my thoughts
Just sink into the night
The tempo of the music
Calms my breathing nice and slow
Time to turn the music up
Relax just let yourself go

The Hunter

Still, almost silent hearing far off traffic
Trees barely moving , sunset moonlight
Lights coming on, night creatures stirring
Ripples on the pond from fish always moving
Here she stalks her prey, watching and waiting
For the right moment, staring through the grass
The time is right, takes her chance
And kills

Looking

Looking out across the endless ocean
A million salty tears you have devoured
Enticing me in with your hypnotic sounds
Always playing a different tune
How many souls have you claimed
Lost in your wondrous depth
Forever riding your moonlight tides
You keep your secrets hidden for eternity

The candle

The light from the candle burns silently
Looking out into the night
Reflecting on the window pane
Guiding souls into the light
The wax slowly starts to melt
A liquid pool starts to form
A gentle fragrance lingers by
Full of memories to keep you warm
The flame starts to die down
The wick begins to cool
The room becomes dark once more
Shadows fade into the walls

Footprints

An abundance of footprints in the snow
Who do they belong to I'll never know
What tales they have to tell I wonder
Secrets they keep inside and ponder
Coexisting for a single moment in time
Pure white becomes full of dirt and grime
Imprinted in this picture for eternity
Rain washes them away, nothing left to see
No memories that there were ever there
No one around to even care
I'll remember though, the patterns made
Where people walked, children once played

Fire

The flames flicker in the wind
Colours of burnt red orange glow
Flames dancing widely twisting and turning
White hot embers crackle below
Beautifully inviting, your touch is forbidden
Tiny sparks widely dance in the air
Like fireflies caught up in a jar
You can't help but look and stare
You have my mind wrapped up in a trance
Keeping me company at night
Until you finally burn yourself out
Your no longer needed in daylight

The web

Like a well constructed building
You hang hazily off the tree
Full of the moist morning dew
You have spun your web eloquently
Your architecture is astounding
So delicately perfect
Scattered dried up corpses are proof
All your hard work was worth it.

Shadows

When the sun is shining bright
Your shadow comes to sight
Connecting light and dark
You never really are apart
Always watching from afar
Silently moving when you are
No face no emotion just empty darkness
No comfort, just staring quite heartless
So close but far away
You can run but it will always stay
Clouds cover the suns path
The shadow escapes from your grasp

The ocean

Waves crashing over the ocean powerful and forbidding
What secrets do they tell locked up inside so tight
Spray cascading in the air forming white bubbles
Withdrawing back into the sea fizzing out of sight

Inching closer evermore taking back what belongs
Swallowing up the golden sand bowing at its prey
Rocks tumble and chink and are crushed around
Having no choice but to give in and obey

Far out the inky water is as still as can be
Reflecting off the sunlight like a mirror smooth as glass
Picture perfect lines out on the horizon
Knowing In a heartbeat it can change just as fast

Spring

Spring is on the way at last
Cold winter is banished away
Fed up of cold fingers and toes
We don't want you to stay
The cosy nights were magical
Next to the crackling fire
We enjoyed the days of wrapping up
Those times will never tire
Sparking snow that gracefully fell
Turned green to icing white
Snowmen building and sledding what fun
Snow angels in the night
But now it's getting somewhat a bore
Days are too short and cold
Snow drops emerging silently
For warmer days untold

The wonderer

Off on an adventure into the unknown
Got to find that something makes me want to roam
Deeper in the forest I dare to onward go
Not sure who I next meet will be my friend or foe
The trees are whispering silently talking about me I'm sure
I should turn back but I'm craving more
My head is full of anguish deep within my soul
Need a release and let the good times roll
Just on the way to nowhere wonder where I'll go
I'll let the wind guide me to where rivers flow
Following my feet, birds soaring so high
To the end of the beginning I'll keep on walking by

Wind

An invisible force races along
Gaining momentum powerful and strong
Doesn't care what in is in his path
Wraps round tress and blades of grass
Reaching out with its endless fingers
Branches are moving when it lingers
Neat styled hair is pulled to shreds
What every other woman dreads
Stay out of it away and it will dissipate
Not going anywhere. I'll just sit and wait

Time

We all want to own you
Have you for ourselves
Want to steal precious moments
Those ones what were heartfelt
We could go back to the crossroads
Where which we stood upon
Ponder on the decisions we chose
Think about where we went wrong
Would an hour be enough
To revisit and rewrite
To pick out the good from the bad
This time get it right
But think about who are today
That person would be gone for good
Time has made you who you are
Would you change it all if you could
Don't wish it away it goes quick enough
But to slow it down would be nice
So I could appreciate family and friends
It would be a truly wonderful life

The storm

Grey storm clouds
Tearing across the sky
A blanket full of emotions
Fiercely flying by
Thick with angry torment
Dumping your rain of salty tears
Please let the sun burn a hole in you
And take away the fears
Thinning out slowly
The sky starts to turn blue
Calm is coming, the storm has past
Everywhere is peaceful too

Memories

Where do all our memories go
The ones we cherish so much
If we don't keep them alive
Do we lose the ones we love
Some we keep close and reflect on daily
Others are locked tight away
The ones we choose not to keep
Are just thrown away
Memories can be bad as well
They fill our mind with sorrow
We can try to replace them all
With memories of tomorrow
The worst ones that we shouldn't keep
Are the ones that are full of regret
Let those go, don't let them back
Try your best to forget
Happy memories are there to stay
They are all what they seem
And as for all the rest of them
Keep safe within your dreams

Stillness

In a field stood alone
Without my laptop or my phone
No shoes upon my feet
Helps me hear the earths heart beat
It's silent but it's not
My mind is noisy of things forgot
I shut my eyes to concentrate
To give my brain a well earned break
The wind is dying down
Leaves stop falling to the ground
Calm starts to surround by body
I begin to feel less foggy

Rain

Heavy rain falling spatters on my window
Drips sliding down changing all the time
Tear drop crystals sparking and reflecting
Hypnotising tapping makes a little rhyme
Plants looks clean, natures little shower
No dust in the air, it's all been washed away
Petals looking polished reflecting in puddles
Everything looks clean ready to start the day
Air smells fresher and colours look brighter
Sun comes out a rainbow adorns the sky
Kaleidoscope of colours stretching for miles
After the rain a welcome sight for my eyes

At night

Sun goes down, colours adorn the sky
Cascading around the human eye
Darkness comes and steals it away
Until the start of a brand new day
Look up into the sky at night
Worlds untold, stars so bright
Silently still, the stars do shine
Everlasting lost in time
It's calm, so still, so beautiful
Moonlight shines, nature's light ball

One day

One day when I'm old and grey
I'll look back on my time
Remember all the good times I had
Oh, the memories were just fine
The times I cried myself to sleep
Far too many to recall
They now seem so pointless
Now I'm stuck in these four walls
Count your blessing while you can
Be grateful for every minute
This life you got only one chance
Stand up, be happy and wing it

Lightning Source UK Ltd.
Milton Keynes UK
UKHW02f0614250918
329480UK00006B/823/P